21st Century
Skills Library

ROAD TO RECOVERY

WHOOPING CRANE

Susan H. Gray

Cherry Lake Publishing
Ann Arbor, Michigan

CHERRY LAKE Publishing

Published in the United States of America by Cherry Lake Publishing
Ann Arbor, MI
www.cherrylakepublishing.com

Content Adviser: Tom Stehn, Whooping Crane Coordinator, U.S. Fish and Wildlife
Service, Austwell, Texas

Photo Credits: Pages 4, 5, and 16, © Dan Guravich/Corbis; page 6, © Reuters/
Corbis; page 8, © Arthur Morris/Corbis; page 12, © Academy of Natural Sciences of
Philadelphia/Corbis; pages 18 and 26, © Tom Bean/Corbis; page 22, © Annie Griffiths
Belt/Corbis

Map by XNR Productions Inc.

Library of Congress Cataloging-in-Publication Data
Gray, Susan Heinrichs.
  Whooping crane / by Susan H. Gray.
    p. cm. — (The road to recovery)
  ISBN-13: 978-1-60279-034-6 (hardcover)
  ISBN-10: 1-60279-034-5 (hardcover)
  1. Whooping crane—Juvenile literature. I. Title. II. Series.
  QL696.G84G75 2008
  598.3'2—dc22   2007005149

*Cherry Lake Publishing would like to acknowledge the work of
The Partnership for 21st Century Skills.
Please visit www.21stcenturyskills.org for more information.*

TABLE OF CONTENTS

FIRST FLIGHT

Three tall whooping cranes walk together in a marsh.

It is a cool, crisp morning. A small aircraft rolls down the runway. Little

whooping cranes trot after it. The craft turns and rolls back in the other

direction. The cranes hop up and down, turn, and chase it again. The craft turns once more and speeds up a little. Then it slowly takes to the air.

The cranes run as fast as their legs can carry them. Then they spread their wings and flap. They rise into the air, staying with the craft. Soon the little

Humans affect the survival of other species in ways you might not expect. In Texas, humans and whooping cranes at times compete for fresh water. When the cranes migrate, the leading cause of death is colliding with power lines. And sometimes hunters mistakenly or illegally shoot the cranes.

But humans aren't always the enemy. People have made great efforts to save the whooping crane. Can you think of efforts that humans have made to help other species?

Whooping cranes take to the sky, showing their black wing tips.

aircraft returns to the runway, and the cranes do the same. They have just finished their first flying lesson!

This pilot flies a lightweight aircraft as part of an effort to teach whooping cranes how to fly south in the winter.

CHAPTER TWO

THE WHOOPING CRANE'S LIFE

Adult whooping cranes are taller than most fifth graders!

Whooping cranes live only in the United States and Canada. They are large, long-legged birds. They are the tallest birds in North America.

Adult cranes stand 5 feet (1.5 meters) tall. They weigh around 15 pounds (6.8 kilograms). This is about the same as a large house cat.

The whooping crane has a long beak that it uses to catch food.

Except for a few places, their feathers are snowy white. They have short

black feathers on the face. Their wing tips are also black.

The birds feed in ponds and wet areas. They have long beaks—perfect

for snatching food from the water. They eat crayfish, frogs, crabs, clams, and fish. They also eat berries, insects, small birds, snakes, mice, corn, wheat, and other crops during migration.

Whooping cranes are known for their courtship dances. Before mating, males and females will dance, hop, run, flap their wings, and "whoop" at each other. Cranes form lifelong pairs. If one crane dies, the other will find a new mate.

Females usually lay two eggs. Normally, the first chick to hatch will survive. The second chick, however, might not make it. This is because there may not be enough food for it. Or a **predator** might carry it away.

Whooping cranes, of course, are members of the crane family. There are 15 different species of cranes. All are tall birds with long legs. Many have beautiful feathers on their heads or necks. They do complicated dances to attract mates. Cranes are found all over the world except in South America and Antarctica. In some countries, they are symbols of a long life.

A whooping crane mother stands next to her darker chick at the International Crane Foundation in Baraboo, Wisconsin.

Chicks are reddish brown in color. Their feathers are soft and downy.

At about four months, white feathers begin to appear.

Some cranes are big travelers and some are not. This is because some

flocks migrate and some don't.

There are three flocks of whooping cranes in North America. One flock migrates back and forth between Texas and Canada. One flock goes between Florida and Wisconsin. The third flock stays in Florida year-round.

The two migrating flocks spend their summers in the north. They build nests, lay eggs, and raise their young. In the fall, they head south to escape the cold winter. The young birds fly with their parents. This is how they learn the route. The cranes spend their winters in warm southern states where food is abundant. When spring comes, they fly north again.

21st Century Content

In 1973, the U.S. Congress passed the Endangered Species Act (ESA). It forbids any government organization, corporation, or citizen from harming endangered animals. It also protects their habitats.

The ESA protects only species officially listed as threatened or endangered. Ordinary citizens like you can ask the government to include an animal on the list. Since being placed on the endangered species list, the whooping crane population has increased by hundreds.

CHAPTER THREE

A SMALL GROUP GETS EVEN SMALLER

American naturalist John James Audubon painted this whooping crane for a book he completed in 1835 called The Birds of America.

Early North American explorers wrote about whooping cranes. They saw flocks in Mexico, the United States, and Canada. However, crane numbers were never very high. In the 1860s, there were probably no more than 1,400 birds.

The slightest disturbance can cause great harm to such a small group. This fact is especially true of whooping cranes. Most pairs raise only one baby each year. So the number of cranes does not increase quickly. One disaster can wipe out dozens of birds in a season. Then it takes years for the population to build back up.

This is what happened to the whooping cranes. For about 100 years, they faced one problem after another. From the mid-1800s to the mid-1900s, their numbers shrank to almost nothing. What caused this to happen?

Hunting was part of the problem. Whooping cranes have beautiful feathers. People loved to wear hats decorated with them. Some people also were egg collectors. They enjoyed owning the eggs of rare birds. Every time a bird was killed and every time an egg was taken, the crane population dropped.

Resting in shallow water like this reed bed protects whooping cranes from predators.

A bigger problem, though, had to do with the cranes' habitat.

Whooping cranes live in wet areas. Even when they migrate, they stop and

rest at ponds and muddy spots. At night, they stand in shallow water to be

safe from predators.

Over the years, these wetlands disappeared. Many were drained or filled in with dirt. Some areas were turned into croplands. Others were built up into towns and cities. Places where the cranes fed and made nests disappeared.

In some cases, scientists made things even worse. They saw the cranes disappearing and hurried to get eggs and skins for their museums and for research.

Learning & Innovation Skills

Whooping cranes eat many different kinds of foods—berries, insects, mice, and more. When they eat berries, they are eating plant seeds. These seeds wind up in the birds' droppings. When the cranes move about, they spread the seeds to new areas.

When the cranes eat small animals, they help keep those animal populations under control. Cranes themselves become the food of other animals, including foxes, wolves, coyotes, raccoons, and bobcats. Sometimes these animals eat the eggs or baby cranes. As terrible as this seems, it may actually be helpful. When food is scarce, the parent cranes have trouble feeding their two babies. But if one egg or hatchling disappears, the other has a better chance of surviving.

This is all part of nature's cycle. One species affects the survival of another. In what ways do humans—do you—participate in this cycle?

The whooping crane population has always been at risk because of its small numbers. These two adults feed in a Texas bay.

In time, there were only two small flocks left. One flock lived year-

round in Louisiana. The other flock migrated between Texas and Canada.

In 1941, the Louisiana flock was down to six birds.

In the Texas flock, only 15 remained.

In 1941, things got even worse. Bad weather had destroyed the Louisiana flock. The whooping cranes in Texas were the last ones on Earth. That year, only three of four crane pairs were old enough to lay eggs and raise young.

Learning & Innovation Skills

Whooping cranes might travel many thousands of miles in their lives. They can live to be more than 30 years old. Can you think of any other animals that travel as much during their lifetime?

CHAPTER FOUR

A LONG, SLOW RECOVERY

In 1937, the U.S. government took the first step in saving the cranes.

The government created a safe place in Texas. This was the Aransas

The Aransas National Wildlife Refuge in Texas became a protected
land for many birds, including whooping cranes, in 1937.

National Wildlife Refuge. It was not just for

whooping cranes. It was for many different kinds

of birds—especially ducks and geese.

At that time, people knew cranes spent the winter

there. But no one knew where they spent the summer.

It was a mystery where they went to lay their eggs.

Finally, in the summer of 1954, whooping cranes

were spotted in a national park in Canada. This was

great news. Now people could protect the cranes in their

winter *and* summer homes. They could protect the eggs.

They could plan how to raise the crane numbers.

Experts knew that the cranes usually laid two

eggs. They also knew that often just one chick

Every winter, the whooping cranes find a safe home in southern Texas at the Aransas National Wildlife Refuge. It is one of more than 540 National Wildlife Refuges across the United States. These refuges are managed by the U.S. Fish and Wildlife Service. This governmental organization's Web site—www.fws.gov— has lots of information about protecting animals and their habitats.

*Adult sandhill cranes walk with their two-day-old chick in Florida. A
project that involved this species helping to raise whooping cranes failed.*

survived. So they began to visit the nests. They took one egg from each

nest. They kept those eggs warm and hatched them.

In the meantime, the parent birds raised the other hatchling. Over the years, many birds grew up in captivity. Their brothers and sisters grew up in the wild.

This was all part of a plan. The whole plan was to use the captive birds to build up the Texas–Canada flock and to start new flocks. Crane experts had different ideas about how to make this happen. Some ideas worked, but some did not.

One idea had to do with sandhill cranes. These birds look a lot like whooping cranes but are grayish brown. Scientists began putting whooping crane eggs into sandhill nests. The baby whoopers hatched, and sandhill parents took care of them. Little whoopers followed them on migrations. Everything seemed to be going well.

However, when the whooping cranes became adults, problems arose. They were not interested in the other whooping cranes. They did not know how to choose whoopers for mates. The scientists knew they needed to try

something else.

In 1993, scientists started a whole new flock in Florida. They brought

in baby cranes that had hatched in captivity. The birds were not taught to

*Researchers and veterinarians care for whooping
cranes as part of a program in Maryland.*

migrate. They stay in Florida year-round. These cranes now build nests and lay their own eggs. By 2006, the flock had grown to more than 50 birds.

In 2001, a third flock was started in Wisconsin. This group was part of a big experiment. The flock began with chicks raised in captivity. Experts hoped to teach them to migrate to Florida and back. But how could people teach birds where to fly? The people would have to fly! And that's what is happening today.

Here's how it works. Scientists in Maryland take care of whooping crane eggs. They play recordings to the eggs. These recordings are the sounds of adult cranes and the sounds of **ultralight** aircraft motors running. By the time the chicks hatch, they know these sounds.

Soon the chicks get to see an ultralight aircraft. They watch the aircraft circle their pen, and they chase after it because the pilot is giving them treats.

Operation Migration is one group that helps carry out the ultralight project. One of the men who started Operation Migration is Bill Lishman. When Bill was a boy, he wanted to be a pilot. But he found out he was color-blind, and therefore not allowed to fly regular airplanes. He didn't let that stop him from pursuing his career. Instead, he learned to fly ultralights! In 1988, he became the first pilot to lead a flock of birds. The movie *Fly Away Home* is based on his success. Operation Migration's pilots have taught Canada geese, sandhill cranes, and whooping cranes how to migrate.

This way, the chicks get used to following the aircraft. Soon they are chasing it through an open field. When they are about 50 days old, the chicks travel in a box to Wisconsin, where they begin flight lessons.

Finally, the day comes to fly south. The pilot climbs into the ultralight and starts the motor. As he takes off into the sky, the birds follow. They do not know it, but they are making their first migration. They are on their way to Florida for the winter.

It takes weeks to reach Florida. But the trip is worth it. The young cranes learn the route quite well. The next spring, they return to Wisconsin on their own without the ultralight.

CHAPTER FIVE

WHOOPING CRANES TODAY

Today, scientists must keep a careful count of the endangered whooping cranes to make sure that populations continue to grow.

Every year, scientists count all the whooping cranes. They find out how many birds are in the Texas–Canada group. They count the Wisconsin–Florida birds. They count the Florida birds that do not migrate. And they count the birds in captivity.

In 2006, crane numbers were up to 518. This was great news, but the work goes on. The goal is to have more than 1,000 birds. Experts hope to reach that point by the year 2035.

At one time, whooping cranes were just a few nesting females away from dying out completely. Experts, public officials, and ordinary citizens have worked together to put the species on the road to recovery.

Power lines are a new threat to whooping cranes migrating south.

Operation Migration goes on every year, too. New whoopers are learning their migration route every fall. All is not perfect, though. Sometimes, migrating cranes die. They fly into power lines and into fences. Some of their resting spots are becoming polluted. So now people are trying to protect these stopover points.

When whooping cranes were in serious trouble in the 1950s, some concerned people started a whooper club. Members of this club were pen pals across the United States and Canada. They worked together on ways to help the whooping cranes and urged the governments of both their countries to work together, too.

In 1961, the club became the Whooping Crane Conservation Association. Today, the group continues to work with government and the public to protect the whooping cranes.

People are also working to protect the Aransas Refuge. It seems that cranes would be out of harm's way on a refuge. After all, a refuge is created to be a safe place. Rivers and streams flow into the refuge. They provide water for the wildlife there.

However, cities need water more than ever and take the water from those rivers and streams. People are working out ways to share this water. They hope to ensure that humans and refuge animals all get enough. It is crucial if the whooping crane is to continue its recovery.

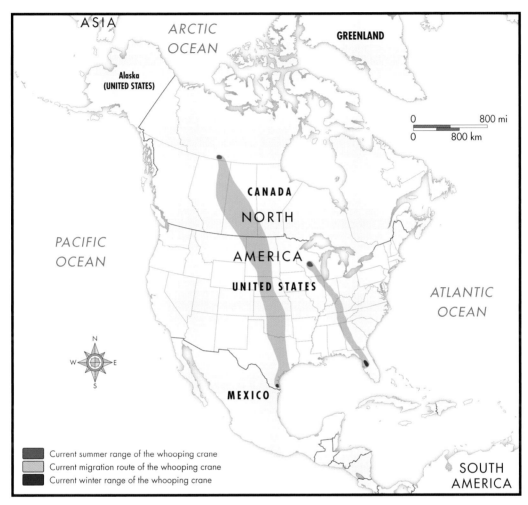

This map shows where the whooping crane lives in North America. It also shows whooping crane migration routes.

Glossary

captivity (kap-TIH-vih-tee) the state of being confined

conservation (kon-sur-VAY-shun) the preservation and protection of environments, animals, or plants

endangered (en-DAYN-jurd) in danger of dying out completely

habitats (HAB-ih-tats) the places where an animal or plant naturally lives and grows

hatchling (HATCH-leeng) an animal that has recently hatched from an egg

migrate (MYE-grate) to travel from one area to another

predator (PREH-duh-tur) an animal that hunts and eats other animals

refuge (REFF-yooj) a shelter or a safe place

species (SPEE-sheez) a group of similar plants or animals

ultralight (UL-truh-lyte) very lightweight; a lightweight aircraft

FOR MORE INFORMATION

Books

Dudley, Karen. *Whooping Cranes*. Austin, TX: Raintree Steck-Vaughn, 1997.

DuTemple, Lesley. *North American Cranes*. Minneapolis: Carolrhoda Books, 1998.

Goodman, Susan E. *Saving the Whooping Crane*. Minneapolis: Millbrook Press, 2008.

Imbriaco, Alison. *The Whooping Crane: Help Save This Endangered Species!* Berkeley Heights, NJ: MyReportLinks.com Books, 2006.

Web Sites

Environmental Education for Kids!—Whooping Crane
www.dnr.state.wi.us/org/caer/ce/eek/critter/bird/crane.htm
For a profile of the life of the whooping crane and information on conservation efforts

International Crane Foundation
www.savingcranes.org
For information about the study and preservation of whooping cranes

Journey North: Whooping Crane
www.learner.org/jnorth/search/Crane.html
To read about the efforts to aid and track whooping crane migration

Operation Migration
www.operationmigration.org
For information on using ultralight aircraft to lead whooping crane migration

INDEX

ABOUT THE AUTHOR

Susan H. Gray has a master's degree in zoology. She has written more than 70 science and reference books for children and especially loves writing about animals. Gray also likes to garden and play the piano. She lives in Cabot, Arkansas, with her husband, Michael, and many pets.